From Budgets to Balance Sheets:

A Manager's Introduction to Finance

Bonnie Knapp

American Media Publishing
4900 University Avenue
West Des Moines, Iowa 50266-6769
1-800-262-2557

From Budgets to Balance Sheets:
A Manager's Introduction to Finance

Bonnie Knapp
Copyright © 1997 by American Media Inc.

This publication is designed to provide accurate and authoritative information in regard to the subject matter covered. It is sold with the understanding that neither the author nor the publisher is engaged in rendering legal, accounting, or other professional service. If legal advice or other expert assistance is required, the services of a competent professional should be sought.

Credits:
American Media Publishing: Art Bauer
                                Todd McDonald

Managing Editor: Karen Massetti Miller
Designer: Gayle O'Brien
Cover Design: Polly Beaver

Published by American Media Inc.
4900 University Avenue
West Des Moines, IA 50266-6769

Library of Congress Catalog Card Number 97-073104
Knapp, Bonnie
From Budgets to Balance Sheets: A Manager's Guide to Finance

Printed in the United States of America
1997
ISBN 1-884926-77-0

Introduction

A strange phenomenon occurs in the intellectual development of a number of business professionals. Though we are articulate, knowledgeable, and competent in our subject areas, we discover that our minds turn to mush when we face the prospect of dealing with "numbers." How many times have your heard a colleague say, "Oh, I just hate numbers. Give me words and pictures and I'm okay" or "My brain shuts down on all that financial stuff!" If you are reading this book, maybe you've said or thought something similar.

The intent of this book is to break through the mystique of financial management by turning numbers into simple words and pictures. The book is not all-inclusive, nor is it intended to make you an expert. If it does nothing more than help you understand what questions to ask about those numbers, it will have been successful.

Read this book one piece at a time, and take time to think about the material. Get your hands on some financial reports and dissect them, using the book as a guide. Figure out what tools can be useful to your team or department and delve into them. Only by doing this—by facing those numbers head on—will you begin to internalize financial management and ultimately use it effectively in your work.

As a small-business owner, I have come to crave those numbers and reports even though my background is primarily in "words and pictures." Though I usually have a general idea of how my business is doing, financial management provides me with a necessary reality check. It helps me get an accurate reflection of my business, and more importantly, it helps me decide where to invest my money and what goals to set—as it should.

About the Author

Bonnie Knapp is a consultant and small-business entrepreneur who faces the realities of financial management on a daily basis. A long-time member of the "I hate numbers" school, she quickly learned the intricacies of financial management.

Bonnie has spent the past 10 years as a training and organization development consultant and a freelance technical writer. In addition to running her retail business, Train of Thought Books, she currently spends a great deal of her consulting work assisting entrepreneurs with small-business development—including the creation of useful financial projections. She received her bachelor's degree from Youngstown State University, earned her master's degree at Bowling Green State University, and did doctoral work at the University of Minnesota.

Table of Contents

Chapter *One*

Financial Management Isn't My Job—Is It?

Chapter Objectives

▶ Clarify the concept of financial management.

▶ Identify the benefits of understanding basic financial management.

▶ Define your responsibilities in managing the financial aspects of your business.

The world of financial management can seem overwhelming unless you understand its basics, but once you do, the mystique disappears.

Do you cringe when someone starts talking about the P&L? assets and liabilities? direct and indirect costs? Do you feel a weight on your shoulders when the finance department asks you about factory burden or manufacturing overhead? Does your head spin at the mere mention of ROI or cash flow analysis or equity? If so, relax. You are fairly normal. The world of financial management can seem overwhelming unless you understand its basics, but once you do, the mystique disappears.

Who *Is* Responsible for Financial Management?

Many companies insulate their employees from the financial aspects of the business. Some managers do it because they feel it is their own responsibility and that their employees have enough other matters to concern them. Others don't believe their employees will understand the intricacies of financial statements, or perhaps they themselves don't understand them. And still others feel the more information they disclose—even within the company itself—the greater the chance important information will find its way into competitors' hands.

1

So the answer to the question "Who's responsible for financial management?" seems easy, doesn't it? Financial management in organizations is something an accountant does, or the finance department, or at the very least, the president of the company. After all, they are responsible for that part of the business. You are responsible for producing a product, providing customer service, keeping track of inventory, or some other equally important part of the business. Right?

Well, maybe not.

Take a Moment

Think about it for a minute. Aren't you and your work group expected to contribute to the financial well-being of your organization in some way? Here is a list of ways that members of an organization typically contribute to that organization's financial health—check those that apply to you.

❏   Improve productivity

❏   Reduce costs

❏   Stay within budget

❏   Other_____

What Is Financial Management?

You do have a role in your organization's financial management.

Perhaps by now you're beginning to see that you do have a role in your organization's financial management. But it's hard to take responsibility for something if you don't really know what it is, and financial management is no exception. So just what is financial management, anyway? One of the easiest ways to define *financial management* is to think of it as a cyclical process, as illustrated by Figure 1.

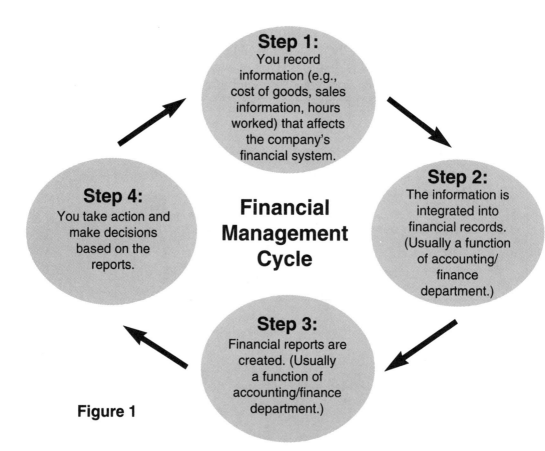

Figure 1

8

Financial management begins when a person within the organization records information that affects the company's financial system (Step 1 in Figure 1). That person can be anyone in the organization who is expected to contribute to the financial well-being of the company—namely *you*. That information is then integrated into the organization's financial records by the accounting or finance department (Step 2). That department creates financial reports (Step 3) that members of the organization use to make decisions that affect the organization (Step 4). The level of those decisions varies from person to person, as does the amount and type of information each one receives. Nevertheless, financial information is necessary for good decision making at every level of the organization.

Everyone Is Responsible

As Figure 1 illustrates, every member of an organization is responsible for financial management. While the president of the company is responsible for deciding in which product lines she will invest, the janitor is responsible for ordering the most economical cleaning supplies, and the training manager needs to review the cost of paper and reproduction costs for training materials. By understanding basic financial management tools and terms, every employee in the organization can have a fiscal conscience. Consider the following example:

> By understanding basic financial management tools and terms, every employee in the organization can have a fiscal conscience.

■ Mariah has been with the company for about three months now. She was hired into the Training Department to develop leadership curriculum and the ensuing courses for senior-level managers in the organization. The department Mariah joined was responsible for three different divisions within the corporation, all of which had different senior management. As Mariah worked on the leadership curriculum that would ultimately consist of classes to be presented in different locations across the United States, she tried to establish boundaries for herself.

She had done a good job of determining the needs of the organization and its managers during her first three months on the job; now she needed to start developing courses and looking for existing resources. She had found a computer simulation that addressed some of the core skills that managers at the company needed, but it seemed expensive to Mariah. She went to her team leader, Jim, to discuss the

1

budget for this project. She explained to Jim about the course she wanted to review and shared her concerns about the cost. "If you could give me the budget that was developed last year for this effort, it would really help me make some decisions."

Jim laughed and shook his head. "Oh, Mariah, don't worry about the cost. Our budget is paid for by Division X right now."

"Yeah, so what does that mean, Jim?"

"It means Division X is fat—they're doing great and have lots of money, so for the most part, we don't have to worry about our costs. They cover just about everything we ask for these days," Jim explained. "I'll check to see how much we forecast for this project. I think it was about $20,000, but I'm not sure. In the meantime, just do what you think is right and don't get hung up on the budget."

Take a Moment

Suggested answers are on page 88.

1. What problems might arise because of Jim's answer to Mariah?

   _____

   _____

   _____

2. What could potentially happen to the Training Department if Division X faces financial difficulties?

   _____

   _____

   _____

3. How might Jim and his team avoid that fate?

   _____

   _____

Understanding Financial Management Brings Benefits

In her quest for some definition of costs and budget, Mariah addressed some of the key benefits that come from understanding and using the basics of financial management. In Mariah's case, having financial information would have helped her make sound decisions about costs.

Understanding the basics of financial management provides many advantages:

◆ It provides a basis for intelligent decision making.

◆ It can increase profits.

◆ It can be used as a tool for improvement (measurement).

◆ It builds ownership across the organization.

Understanding financial management can help managers decide whether their daydreaming about new equipment, new systems, or innovative new products is rooted in reality. An idea that may be sound when the company has excess funds can be disastrous when the business is expanding.

Understanding financial management can help make your employment within your organization more secure. As we discussed earlier, you are expected to contribute to your organization's financial health in some way, such as improving productivity, reducing costs, and staying within your budget. Understanding financial management will help you understand and meet your company's expectations in these areas, which will increase your value to your organization. You will also have a better understanding of how you and your department contribute to your company's bottom line—and be able to explain that contribution to others in the organization.

Companies can survive with centralized financial management in which only the president of the company or the chief financial officer knows the details—especially if they have a product for which there is a strong need and a solid customer base—but such companies may not thrive in the long term. They may miss opportunities. And if the need for a product changes or the customers decide they need something else, managers may not know where the company's money is invested, how much inventory is available, or how much cash is available for expansion.

> **Understanding financial management can help managers decide whether their daydreaming about new equipment, new systems, or innovative new products is rooted in reality.**

11

Take a Moment

Think about how you make decisions. Are you given the information you need to manage your part of the business effectively? Do you know how you can make a difference? Are you clear about the ways in which you can have an impact on the bottom line of the company? Do you have to depend on someone else to give you the information you need, or can you track it yourself?

What financial information related to your part of the business do you receive regularly? How often do you get it? What do you do with the information?

Information about the . . .	What information do you receive?	How often?	How do you use the information?
Project			
Department or Division			
Company			

What financial information related to your part of the business do you wish you received regularly? How often would you need it? What would you do with it?

What information do you wish you received?	How often?	How would you use the information?

Chapter Summary

Every member of an organization is responsible for that organization's financial management. Understanding the basics of financial management provides many advantages:

- ◆ It provides a basis for intelligent decision making.

- ◆ It can increase profits.

- ◆ It can be used as a tool for improvement (measurement).

- ◆ It builds ownership across the organization.

We can think of financial management as a cycle that begins when a person within the organization records information that affects the company's financial system. That information is then integrated into the organization's financial records by the accounting or finance department. That department creates financial reports that members of the organization use to make decisions that affect the organization.

Financial information is necessary for good decision making at every level of the organization. While the president of the company is responsible for deciding in which product lines she will invest, the janitor is responsible for ordering the most economical cleaning supplies, and the training manager needs to review the cost of paper and reproduction costs for training materials. By understanding basic financial management tools and terms, every employee in the organization can have a fiscal conscience—and increase their value to the organization in the process.

Self-Check: Chapter 1 Review

Answers to the following questions are on page 88.

1. Who is responsible for financial management within an organization?

   _____

   _____

2. List four advantages of understanding financial management.

   a. _____

   _____

   b. _____

   _____

   c. _____

   _____

   d. _____

   _____

3. Financial management may be thought of as a cycle consisting of four steps. What are the steps?

   Step 1: _____

   Step 2: _____

   Step 3: _____

   Step 4: _____

4. What is your role in the financial management cycle?

_____

_____

_____

1

Chapter *Two*

Tracking Performance with Balance Sheets and Income Statements

Chapter Objectives

▶ Define common terms of financial management.

▶ Understand the balance sheet and the income statement.

▶ Describe the need for a cash flow analysis.

Before you can make intelligent financial decisions and really know how your performance impacts your company, you should understand some of the universal concepts and tools of financial management. Fortunately, financial management uses standard financial reports that vary only by the level of detail into which they go. This section will describe the *balance sheet* and the *income statement* (also known as the *profit and loss* statement or the *P&L*).

The Balance Sheet and Its Components

The *balance sheet* (Figure 2) is a financial snapshot of your company at a given point in time, usually at the end of a month, a quarter, or the fiscal year. It shows the business's financial status at that point in time and helps you see your *assets,* or what you have, and your *liabilities,* or what you owe on that day. As the word *balance* suggests, the total assets on the balance sheet should equal the total liabilities plus the *net worth,* or the owner's equity in the business. (The term *net* means after deductions. In this case, *net worth* refers to the owner's equity in the business after liabilities are deducted.)

The *balance sheet* is a financial snapshot of your company at a given point in time.

Because the balance sheet shows the financial status of your business at a particular point in time, you can compare a current balance sheet to previous balance sheets to see how much your business has improved or declined. The balance sheet can also be a starting point for developing plans to take your company into the future.

Often compiled at the end of an accounting period, the balance sheet for all companies consists of the same categories presented in the same order. The amount of detail (shown in subcategories on the balance sheet) varies depending on the needs of the company.

2

Assets			Liabilities	
Current Assets		$_____	Current Liabilities	$_____
Fixed Assets	$_____		Long-Term Liabilities	$_____
Less Accumulated Depreciation	$_____		**Total Liabilities**	$_____
Net Fixed Assets		$_____		
Other Assets		$_____	**Net Worth**	$_____
Total Assets		$_____	**Total Liabilities and Net Worth**	$_____

Figure 2

The *assets* are anything of value that is owned or legally due the business. They are listed in high to low order of liquidity on the left side or the top half of the balance sheet. *Liquidity* refers to the ability you have to convert assets to cash. Those assets that are most liquid and can easily become spendable cash are listed first. As you might guess, cash is the number one liquid asset.

Assets are anything of value that is owned or legally due the business.

Liabilities are debts and monetary obligations.

The *liabilities,* which include debts and monetary obligations, are listed on the right side or the bottom half of the balance sheet. Whereas the assets are listed in order of decreasing liquidity, the liabilities are listed by immediacy. Those that are due sooner are listed first, followed by the more long-term debts.

To see how these elements work together, let's complete a balance sheet for a hypothetical company called Calley Construction.

Determining Your Assets

Current Assets

Current assets include cash and other assets that could easily be turned into cash within one year.

We'll begin at the top of the assets column (see Figure 3). *Current assets* include cash and other assets that could easily be turned into cash within one year:

◆ Cash—Money in checking and savings accounts.

◆ Petty cash—Funds for miscellaneous expenditures.

◆ Accounts receivable—Money owed (by someone other than officers or employees) for services or merchandise but not yet collected.

◆ Short-term investments—Marketable securities, certificates of deposit, etc.

◆ Inventory/Supplies—Raw materials and supplies on hand, work in progress, and all finished goods.

◆ Prepaid expenses—Goods, benefits, or services you buy or rent in advance, e.g., office supplies, insurance, space.

As you can see on the next page, Calley has $21,500 in current assets. This includes $10,000 in accounts receivable from customers who have not yet paid them for their services. It also includes $5,000 that Calley has invested in supplies that will enable them to do future construction jobs. (Since Calley has no short-term investments, none are shown on the balance sheet.)

Assets		
Current Assets		
Cash		$ 3,500
Petty cash		$ 500
Accounts receivable		$10,000
Inventory/supplies		$ 5,000
Prepaid expenses		$ 2,500
Total Current Assets		$21,500

Figure 3

Fixed Assets

Below the current assets on the left-hand side of the balance sheet come the *fixed assets*. These are fairly permanent investments that are necessary for the day-to-day operations of the business and that are not intended for resale. Fixed assets include:

◆ Land (the original purchase price).

◆ Buildings.

◆ Improvements to buildings.

◆ Production equipment.

◆ Office equipment.

◆ Furniture.

◆ Vehicles.

Fixed assets are fairly permanent investments that are necessary for the day-to-day operations of the business.

2

Calley Construction leases a building for office space and equipment storage, so they don't have any land or building assets. Most of their fixed assets appear in the form of equipment and vehicles (see Figure 4).

Assets		
Current Assets		
Cash		$ 3,500
Petty cash		$ 500
Accounts receivable		$ 10,000
Supplies		$ 5,000
Prepaid expenses		$ 2,500
Total Current Assets		$ 21,500
Fixed Assets		
Office furniture	$ 4,000	
Office equipment	$ 10,000	
Construction equipment	$150,000	
Vehicles	$ 32,000	
Total Fixed Assets	$196,000	
Less Accumulated Depreciation	$ 25,000	
Net Fixed Assets		$171,000

Figure 4

Fixed assets that can wear out, such as machinery, equipment, or computers, *depreciate,* or become lower in value, over time. The amount of depreciation is determined by taking the value of each piece of equipment and reducing that value over the equipment's useful life according to a schedule designated by IRS rules. When depreciation is subtracted from total fixed assets (see Figure 4), the result is recorded as *net fixed assets* (remember, the term *net* means after deductions).

2

Deducting depreciation in this way allows companies to set aside money for replacement costs. The dollar figure for depreciation is shown as a reserve amount of money on the books. However, as you will see when we discuss cash flow, it is not an actual cash expenditure, so it is actually available cash.

Other Assets

The bottom of the assets column shows *other assets* the company might hold (see Figure 5). These include long-term investments, such as stocks and bonds that are owned for investment purposes, and intangible assets, such as patents or copyrights.

As you look at all the items in the assets column, remember: Assets are shown at their original purchase price regardless of their current value on the market.

Balance Sheets and Income Statements

Assets		
Current Assets		
Cash		$ 3,500
Petty cash		$ 500
Accounts receivable		$ 10,000
Supplies		$ 5,000
Prepaid expenses		$ 2,500
Total Current Assets		$ 21,500
Fixed Assets		
Office furniture	$ 4,000	
Office equipment	$ 10,000	
Construction equipment	$150,000	
Vehicles	$ 32,000	
Total Fixed Assets	$196,000	
Less Accumulated Depreciation	$ 25,000	
Net Fixed Assets		$171,000
Other Assets		$0
Total Assets		$192,500

Figure 5

Calley Construction has total assets of $192,500.

Determining Your Liabilities

Current Liabilities

Now let's look at the liabilities shown on the right-hand portion of the balance sheet. At the top of the liabilities column are *current liabilities*—those debts and financial obligations that need to be paid within 12 months (see Figure 6). Current liabilities usually include:

♦ Accounts payable—Money owed to suppliers.

♦ Notes payable—Current payment due on long-term debt, including principal and interest.

♦ Payroll—Salaries and wages currently owed.

♦ Taxes payable.

2

Current liabilities are debts and financial obligations that need to be paid within 12 months.

Liabilities		
Current Liabilities		
Accounts payable	$ 4,000	
Current portion due on notes/loan	$ 1,000	
Payroll	$ 3,600	
Taxes payable	$ 5,000	
Total Current Liabilities		$ 13,600

Figure 6

Long-term liabilities include balances on those notes and loans that come due after the current operating year.

Long-Term Liabilities

Below the current liabilities are the long-term liabilities. *Long-term liabilities* include balances on those notes and loans that come due after the current operating year. The outstanding balance minus the current portion is posted on the balance sheet. Examples of long-term liabilities include:

◆ Mortgages.

◆ Bank loans.

◆ Equipment loans.

Calley Construction shows long-term liabilities for loans secured from a finance company for two of their trucks and from a bank for equipment (see Figure 7).

Liabilities		
Current Liabilities		
Accounts payable	$ 4,000	
Current portion due on notes/loan	$ 10,000	
Payroll	$ 3,600	
Taxes payable	$ 5,000	
Total Current Liabilities		$ 13,600
Long-Term Liabilities		
Bank loan	$100,000	
Vehicle loan	$ 4,000	
Total Long-Term Liabilities		$104,000

Figure 7

To complete the liabilities side of the balance sheet, you need to calculate net worth or the owner's equity. This is determined by subtracting the total liabilities from the total assets. Finally, the sum of the total liabilities and the net worth must always equal the total assets, as you can see from the completed balance sheet in Figure 8. In Chapter 4, you will look at some of the basic ways you can use the balance sheet to analyze what's happening in the business.

Calley Construction
Date (month, day, and year)
Balance sheet

Assets			Liabilities		
Current Assets			**Current Liabilities**		
Cash	$ 3,500		Accounts payable	$ 4,000	
Petty cash	$ 500		Current portion due on notes/loan	$ 10,000	
Accounts receivable	$ 10,000		Payroll	$ 3,600	
Supplies	$ 5,000		Taxes payable	$ 5,000	
Prepaid expenses	$ 2,500		*Total Current Liabilities*		$ 13,600
Total Current Assets		$ 21,500	**Long-Term Liabilities**		
Fixed Assets			Bank loan	$100,000	
Office furniture	$ 4,000		Vehicle loan	$ 4,000	
Office equipment	$ 10,000		*Total Long-Term Liabilities*		$104,000
Construction equipment	$150,000				
Vehicles	$ 32,000				
Total Fixed Assets	$196,000				
Less Accumulated Depreciation	-$ 25,000				
Net Fixed Assets		$171,000	**Total Liabilities**		$117,600
Other Assets		$0	Net Worth		$ 74,900
Total Assets		$192,500	**Total Liabilities and Net Worth**		$192,500

Figure 8

Take a Moment

Test your knowledge of balance sheets. Suggested answers are on pages 88 and 89.

1. What is the difference between current and fixed assets?

    _____

2. What is an example of a long-term liability?

    _____

3. How is net worth determined?

    _____

    Look at the balance sheet for Calley Construction:

4. Where are most of the assets invested?

    _____

5. What kinds of fixed assets can be depreciated?

    _____

The *income statement* shows what happened over a period of time.

The Income, or Profit and Loss, Statement

Another important financial tool that probably comes across your desk is the *income statement,* also known as the *P&L,* or *profit and loss statement.* This tool is typically used as a basis for planning and controlling business operations.

While the balance sheet is a snapshot, showing the status of the business at a particular point in time, the income statement shows what happened over a period of time (see Figure 9). For example, Calley Construction might have two balance sheets to compare—one from September 30 and another from the following January 1. While those tools show only the status of the business on those particular dates, the income statement for the period in between shows what happened with expenses and sales/revenue to create changes in the balance sheet.

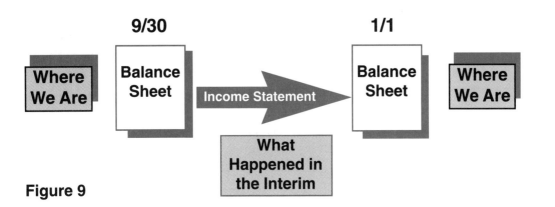

Figure 9

2

What Makes Up the Income Statement?

Four key elements make up the income statement:

◆ Sales/revenue

◆ Cost of goods sold

◆ Operating expenses

◆ Interest expenses

Like the balance sheet, the basic format of the income statement is standardized to make it easier to compare and analyze data. The income statement should always include the time period that is covered and notes explaining any unusual items.

The income statement is used for the following purposes:

◆ To measure the results of operating the business

◆ To figure taxes, borrow money, and sell stock

◆ To find areas that are financial problems (excessive costs or expenses)

◆ To find the greatest profit centers in order to know where to concentrate resources

Basically, the income statement gauges financial progress by comparing the company's *sales and revenue,* or money coming in, with its *expenses,* which are the dollars used to generate the revenue, to determine its *net income,* or the amount of money left after expenses are deducted.

The income statement reflects activity over a period of time, such as a quarter or a year. Figure 10 shows the most basic income statement. The income statement looks at the company's operating performance for a period of time by finding the difference between sales/revenue and the expenses the company incurred to operate. In the case of Calley Construction, the fourth quarter saw $47,224 in sales and revenue—that's money coming in for the company's services. It cost the company $53,137 to get that work done, which left them with a net income of -$5,913.

Calley Construction
Income Statement
for the Quarter Ending December 31

Sales/revenue	**$47,224**
Less expenses	$53,137
Net income	-$5,913

Figure 10

Take a Moment

Put yourself in a management position at Calley Construction. If you worked for a division of the company, what information would you need to see on the income statement in order to improve performance and plan for the future?

_____

_____

_____

_____

2

As you probably realized when you looked at the simplified income statement on page 28, it tells you nothing about wages or salary paid, office expenses, or cost of goods. It tells you nothing about the costs of operating and maintaining the trucks and equipment for the crews. If all you care about is the bottom-line number for net income, this income statement will give you the information you need. However, if you want to do any planning for the future or make improvements, you will need to look at a more detailed income statement. In fact, a detailed income statement can be valuable both as a planning tool, as you will see when we discuss the pro forma income statement, and as a management tool, helping you and your team control the business operations.

A detailed income statement lets you see where the net income came from as well as the expenditures that generated the net income.

A detailed income statement lets you see where the net income came from as well as the expenditures that generated the net income. Let's take a step-by-step look at a more detailed income statement for Calley Construction.

Preparing a Detailed Income Statement

Let's begin our look at a detailed income statement with the company's sales and revenue. Calley Construction provides customers with two different services—earth work and foundation work. The payment they receive for these two types of services is added together on the income statement as sales/revenue (see Figure 11).

Calley Construction
Income Statement
for the Quarter Ending December 31

Earth work	$20,219
Foundation work	$27,005
Sales/Revenue	**$47,224**

Figure 11

Setting out the earth work and foundation work in this way allows the people involved in each area to see what portion of the company's overall revenue they are generating.

The sales/revenue portion of the income statement shows the amount of money taken in. But how much money did the company have to spend to generate this revenue? Calley Construction can use the income statement to determine their *gross profit,* that is, the amount of profit (or loss) when the company's revenue is compared with the cost of goods sold. *Cost of goods sold* refers to the amount of money it cost, including labor and material expenses, to generate the sales/revenue for a particular period of time.

As you can see in Figure 12, Calley Construction generated $47,224 in sales/revenue for the fourth quarter of the year. Their labor costs for both the earth work and foundation work were $34,000 while supplies to be able to do the actual work amounted to $4,987. These two numbers comprise the cost of goods sold. (Notice that salaries for office staff, money for advertising, and other costs that would have to be incurred whether they made those sales or not are figured later under operating expenses.) After you subtract the cost of goods sold from the sales/revenue, you have the *gross profit* for the company. (The term *gross* refers to the amount of profit before deductions are taken.)

Calley Construction
Income Statement
for the Quarter Ending December 31

Earth work	$20,219	
Foundation work	$27,005	
Sales/Revenue	**$47,224**	
Cost of Goods Sold		
Labor Costs		
Earth work	$11,000	
Foundation work	$23,000	
Material		
Earth work	$ 1,000	
Foundation work	$ 3,987	
Gross Profit	**$ 8,237**	

Figure 12

After your figure the gross profit, the next step is to look at the *operating expenses.* You know what the company's direct costs to make the product or deliver the service were, but what were some of the other day-to-day costs? *Operating expenses* are the costs of running the company except for income tax, expenses that come out of financing needs, and those directly related to making the product or delivering the service. Operating expenses include:

◆ Office staff salaries.

◆ Sales expenses.

◆ Advertising expenses.

◆ General administrative expenses.

◆ Other miscellaneous expenses.

Operating expenses also include depreciation on production and office equipment. Calley Construction's operating expenses are shown in Figure 13.

Calley Construction
Income Statement
for the Quarter Ending December 31

Earth work	$20,219
Foundation work	$27,005
Sales/Revenue	**$47,224**
Cost of Goods Sold	
Direct Labor	
Earth work	$11,000
Foundations	$23,000
Material	
Earth work	$ 1,000
Foundations	$ 3,987
Gross Profit	**$ 8,237**
Operating Expenses	
Selling expenses	$ 300
Salaries	$ 6,800
Advertising	$ 300
Other	$ 200
General administrative	$ 300
Depreciation	$ 6,250
Total Operating Expenses	**$14,150**
Income from Operations (Gross profit—total operating expenses)	-$5,913
Interest Expense	-$ 800
Interest Income	$ 0
Income Before Taxes	-$6,713
Income Tax (Refund)	$1,000
Net Income	-$5,713
Net Increase (or Decrease) to Retained Earnings	-$5,713

Figure 13

As you can see, Calley Construction had $14,150 in operating expenses. By subtracting this from the gross profit, you get the income from operations, which, in this case, is -$5,913.

The final step of completing the income statement is to determine the company's *net income,* which is the income after interest expense, interest income, and income taxes have been figured in.

2

Interest expense includes interest paid on any outstanding debt, such as a bank loan. During the fourth quarter, Calley Construction paid $800 in interest expense on their vehicle loans.

Interest income includes interest earned from investments or bank deposits. Calley Construction earned no interest income in the fourth quarter.

Income tax includes state and federal taxes on earnings. Business income taxes are usually figured quarterly. Because Calley Construction showed a negative income from operations in the fourth quarter, they might actually receive a tax refund. The rules for determining tax rates are too complex to describe in detail here, so let's suppose that the company received a $1,000 refund on their quarterly taxes. This will allow us to plug in a number and complete the rest of the balance sheet.

By determining the net income of the company after taxes, you could see how the most recent financial performance affected the company's *retained earnings,* or the amount of money available to the company from past earnings.

Take a Moment

Use your new skills. Suggested answers are on page 89.

1. Using the income statement, what can you tell for sure about the financial performance at Calley Construction during the fourth quarter?

   _____

   _____

2. List some assumptions you might make about Calley Construction in the fourth quarter.

   _____

   _____

Perhaps one of the assumptions you made about the income statement for Calley Construction was that fourth-quarter profits were affected by the seasonal nature of the construction industry. Could a fall/winter slump be responsible for the fourth quarter's negative net income? You can't tell from the single income statement shown. To answer that question, you would need to compare that income statement to others for the rest of the year. Many companies provide managers with comparative income statements and balance sheets so that they can compare current results to the previous year's results.

You could also use a cash flow statement to learn more about Calley Construction's long-term performance. We will learn more about cash flow statements in the following chapter.

Chapter Summary

Financial management uses standard formats that vary only by the level of detail into which they go. Two of the most common tools of financial management are the *balance sheet* and the *income statement* (also known as the profit and loss statement or the P&L).

2

The *balance sheet* is a financial snapshot of your company at a given point in time, usually at the end of a month, a quarter, or the fiscal year, and helps you see your *assets,* or what you have, and your *liabilities,* or what you owe on that day.

The *income statement* helps you see what happened with the business over a period of time. It compares revenue with expenses.

These two tools can help you track the performance of your organization—and your department—and plan for the future.

Self-Check: Chapter 2 Review

Take a few minutes and answer the questions or put the following information in the blank income statement for Laddie's Bookstore, a dealer in new and used books. Suggested answers are on page 89.

1. How much money did the bookstore generate in sales?

    _____

2. The bookstore owner paid a part-time person $1,400 for January, February, and March. Where would that number belong on the income statement?

    _____

3. The bookstore owner purchased $500 worth of used books in the first quarter. Where would you see that number on the income statement? Would that particular topic contain anything else?

    _____

4. The owner spent $300 on a monthly bookstore newsletter for customers. Would that show up on the income statement? If so, where?

    _____

5. Laddie's accountant has done the books and determined that the bookstore owes $2,015 in taxes for the first quarter. Where would she put that number?

    _____

Laddie's Bookstore
Income Statement
for the Quarter Ending March 31

Hardcovers	$54,000
Paperbacks	$21,000
Sales/Revenue	
Cost of Goods Sold	
Direct Labor	
Material	
Gross Profit	
Operating Expenses	
Selling expenses	
Salaries	
Advertising	
Other	
General	
Administrative	
Depreciation	
Total Operating Expenses	
Income from Operations	
(Gross profit—total operating expenses)	
Interest Expense (or income)	
Income Before Taxes	
Income Taxes	
Net Income After Taxes	
Net Increase (or Decrease) to Retained Earnings	

2

Chapter*Three*

Monitoring Cash Flow with Cash Flow Statements

Chapter Objectives

▶ Recognize the need for a cash flow analysis.

▶ Use a cash flow statement to follow cash flow.

The balance sheet and the income statement help you look at the status of the business by showing you the profit and loss or assets and liabilities of the company. The cash flow statement, on the other hand, deals with the actual cash income and expenditures of a business. A cash flow statement:

◆ Shows you how much money you have.

◆ Shows you when you need that money.

◆ Shows you where you will get the money.

Many businesspeople mistakenly believe that *cash flow* and *profit* are synonymous in a business. However, a profitable, or potentially profitable, company can quickly go out of business if the cash flow is not adequate.

> A profitable, or potentially profitable, company can quickly go out of business if the cash flow is not adequate.

Think for a minute of a profitable business as a well-made car. The car is finely tuned, with tires properly inflated. A licensed driver has a map and a clear destination in mind. The driver proceeds on the mapped-out route with everything running smoothly. Suddenly, after several hours on the road, the car sputters and stops. The car, still a well-made vehicle, still with the potential to get the driver to his destination, no longer has the fuel needed to get there. The one thing that made the car go forward is missing, and nothing except gasoline will get it going again.

So it is with a well-made business. Like gasoline for the car, cash is the fuel that keeps a business running. The plan can be in place, the destination mapped out, the manager set to go. Customers appear, the work gets done, the company buys more supplies to be able to do more work, and all seems well. But wait—there's a lag between the time the work is done and the time the customers pay their bills. There's no lag in new customers, though, and no lag in the amount of supplies needed.

The manager spends all available money on supplies to do the new work. But then several customers are late paying their bills, and one doesn't pay at all. Before the manager knows it, there is no extra money to pay the lease on the building or the utilities. He knows it will all be okay once he collects on those accounts receivable, but in the meantime, the business is like that well-made car. It still has the potential to get to the destination. It can still show a profit, but without fuel—or in this case, cash—it will never make it.

If you work for a small company, you are probably very aware of cash flow issues—if not directly, then at least intuitively. When you work for a larger company, however, you may not deal with such issues or even think about them. Either way, understanding the basic concepts will help you better understand company decision making and will also help you with your own decision making.

3

> If you work for a small company, you are probably very aware of cash flow issues.

Take a Moment

Companies deal with cash flow issues in a number of ways. Even if your company does not tell you directly, there may be other ways that you become aware of the current cash flow. What are some of the signs that tell you when cash flow is low?

_____

_____

What are some of the signs that tell you when cash flow is good?

_____

_____

Calculating Cash Flow

Cash flow refers to the amount of cash you have available at a given point in time.

As a first step, let's look at how cash flow is calculated. *Cash flow* refers to your *cash position,* or the amount of cash you have available at a given point in time. It is usually figured on a month-by-month basis. Companies will often juxtapose their actual results with their projections on the cash flow statement so that they can use the statement as a gauge.

A cash flow statement, although filled with enough numbers and figures to make your head spin at first glance, is fairly simple. You start with the cash you had available at the beginning of the month and add any money you received throughout the month (see Figure 14). From this, subtract the money that you pay out to keep the business going. This includes such items such as:

◆ Rent.

◆ Loan payments.

◆ Salaries.

Many of these expenses will be fixed expenses that don't change from month to month. They are constant, unaffected by sales volume or production. You must also include variable expenses, such as advertising, supplies, and so on. The result is the amount of cash on hand you will have for the next month. This amount subtracted from your original amount is your cash position or cash flow.

Cash Flow Is . . .

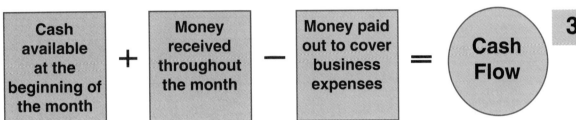

Figure 14

Let's look at Calley Construction again. In order to prepare a cash flow statement, the preparer must have:

◆ Cash available at the beginning of the month.

◆ Cash receipts/sales figures.

◆ The amount spent.

Figure 15 on the following two pages shows how that information was entered in the cash flow statement for Calley Construction's second quarter.

Financials (Projections)	April	May	June	Quarter 2
1. Cash on Hand	10,123	15,865	24,890	50,878
2. Cash Receipts				
(a) Cash Sales	22,691	26,639	30,321	79,651
(b) Collections from Credit Accounts	5,123	6,350	10,214	21,687
(c) Loan or Other Cash Injection (specify)	0	0	0	0
3. Total Cash Receipts	27,814	32,989	40,535	101,338
4. Total Cash Available	37,937	48,854	65,425	152,216
5. Cash Paid Out				
(a) Purchases	6,300	7,500	12,000	25,800
(b) Gross Wages (Excludes withdrawals)	11,333	11,333	11,333	33,999
(c) Payroll Expenses (Taxes, etc.)	113	113	113	339
(d) Outside Services				
(e) Supplies (Office, cleaning, and operating)	125	150	110	385
(f) Repairs and Maintenance	300	650	1,540	2,490
(g) Advertising	400	210	315	925
(h) Car, Delivery, and Travel	1,000	1,541	1,754	4,295
(i) Accounting and Legal			300	300
(j) Rent/Lease	1,000	1,000	1,000	3,000
(k) Telephone	312	318	354	984
(l) Utilities	250	210	198	658
(m) Insurance				
(n) Taxes (real estate, etc.)				
(o) Interest	167	165	163	495
(p) Other Expenses (Specify each)				

(q) Miscellaneous	0			
(r) Subtotal	21,300	23,190	29,180	73,670
(s) Loan Principal Payment	272	274	276	822
(t) Capital Purchases	0			
(u) Other Start-Up Costs	0			
(v) Reserve and/or Escrow (specify)	500	500	500	1,500
(w) Owner's Withdrawal	0			
6. Total Cash Paid Out	22,072	23,964	29,956	75,992
7. Cash Position	15,865	24,890	35,469	76,224
ESSENTIAL OPERATING DATA (Non-cash flow information)				
A. Sales Volume (Dollars)	22,691	26,639	30,321	79,651
by Product Category				
1) Earth work	10,370	11,417	12,911	34,698
2) Foundation work	12,321	15,222	17,410	44,953
B. Accounts Receivable (end of month)				
C. Bad Debt (end of month)				
D. Inventory on Hand (end of month)				
E. Accounts Payable (end of month)				
F. Depreciation				

Figure 15

3

Parts of the Cash Flow Statement

The cash flow statement starts with *cash on hand* (see Figure 16). This refers to your cash position in the preceding month.

Financials (Projections)	April	May	June	Quarter 2
1. Cash on Hand	10,123	15,865	24,890	50,878

Figure 16

Next, cash receipts are recorded. *Cash receipts* means all cash sales. Credit sales do not appear here until they have been converted to cash; then they are recorded in the next row under *collections from credit accounts.* Any other cash that comes into the business, whether from a loan or some other source, is recorded in *loan or other cash injection* (Item 2C). The three amounts under cash receipts are added together to generate the *total cash receipts* for the month (see Figure 17).

Financials (Projections)	April	May	June	Quarter 2
1. Cash on Hand	10,123	15,865	24,890	50,878
2. Cash Receipts				
(a) Cash Sales	22,691	26,639	30,321	79,651
(b) Collections from Credit Accounts	5,123	6,350	10,214	21,687
(c) Loan or Other Cash Injection (specify)	0	0	0	0
3. Total Cash Receipts	27,814	32,989	40,535	101,338

Figure 17

The cash on hand and total cash receipts are then added together for the total cash available. This amount reflects cash available before expenses are taken out. Look at Calley Construction's cash flow figures. How much cash did they have available in the second quarter of the year before expenses? Go to item 4 in Figure 18 and find the total of $152,216.

Financials (Projections)	April	May	June	Quarter 2
1. Cash on Hand	10,123	15,865	24,890	50,878
2. Cash Receipts				0
(a) Cash Sales	22,691	26,639	30,321	79,651
(b) Collections from Credit Accounts	5,123	6,350	10,214	21,687
(c) Loan or Other Cash Injection (specify)	0	0	0	0
3. Total Cash Receipts	27,814	32,989	40,535	101,338
4. Total Cash Available	37,937	48,854	65,425	152,216

Figure 18

Item 5 of the cash flow lists the cash paid out. The total cash paid out appears in item 6 (see Figure 19). Cash paid out covers all expenses, including costs for inventory. Notice that wages and payroll expenses such as payroll taxes and insurance appear separately.

3

● Monitoring Cash Flow with Cash Flow Statements

Financials (Projections)	April	May	June	Quarter 2
1. Cash on Hand	10,123	15,865	24,890	50,878
2. Cash Receipts				
(a) Cash Sales	22,691	26,639	30,321	79,651
(b) Collections from Credit Accounts	5,123	6,350	10,214	21,687
(c) Loan or Other Cash Injection (specify)	0	0	0	0
3. Total Cash Receipts	27,814	32,989	40,535	101,338
4. Total Cash Available	37,937	48,854	65,425	152,216
5. Cash Paid Out				
(a) Purchases	6,300	7,500	12,000	25,800
(b) Gross Wages (excludes withdrawals)	11,333	11,333	11,333	33,999
(c) Payroll Expenses (taxes, etc.)	113	113	113	339
(d) Outside Services				
(e) Supplies (office, cleaning, and operating)	125	150	110	385
(f) Repairs and Maintenance	300	650	1,540	2,490
(g) Advertising	400	210	315	925
(h) Car, Delivery, and Travel	1,000	1,541	1,754	4,295
(i) Accounting and Legal			300	300
(j) Rent/Lease	1,000	1,000	1,000	3,000
(k) Telephone	312	318	354	984
(l) Utilities	250	210	198	658
(m) Insurance				0
(n) Taxes (real estate, etc.)				0
(o) Interest	167	165	163	495
(p) Other Expenses (specify each)				0
(q) Miscellaneous				0
(r) Subtotal	21,300	23,190	29,180	73,670
(s) Loan Principal Payment	272	274	276	822
(t) Capital Purchases				0
(u) Other Start-Up costs				0
(v) Reserve and/or Escrow (specify)	500	500	500	1,500
(w) Owner's Withdrawal				0
6. Total Cash Paid Out	22,072	23,964	29,956	75,992
7. Cash Position	15,865	24,890	35,469	76,224

Figure 19

Cash paid out consists of expenses in the following categories:

a) **Purchases:** Merchandise for resale that you paid for in the current month. This includes merchandise you may have used to make a product.

b) **Gross Wages:** Base pay plus overtime. This is the salary or hourly rate that you pay employees.

c) **Payroll Expenses:** Don't forget paid vacations, sick leave, health insurance, unemployment insurance, etc., here.

3

d) **Outside Services:** Labor on material for special work. For example, if Calley Construction needed to hire another construction company to do part of the work for them, that subcontracting amount would show up here.

e) **Supplies:** Items you purchase to use in the business. These are not for resale.

f) **Repairs and Maintenance:** This includes any large expenses that are expended periodically.

g) **Advertising:** This one speaks for itself. Comparing this figure with your sales volume might be a good measure to use.

h) **Car, Delivery & Travel:** Employee travel expenses go here.

i) **Accounting & Legal:** This refers to outside services the company uses.

j) **Rent/Lease:** This figure reflects money spent for real estate.

k) **Telephone:** What more needs to be said?

l) **Utilities:** Water, heat, electricity—whatever the company pays.

m) **Insurance:** Includes business property and products, as well as worker's compensation.

n) **Taxes:** This includes real estate tax, sales tax, excise tax, etc.

o) **Interest:** Interest for any outstanding loans.

p) **Other Expenses:** Includes monthly payments on equipment that is leased or rented.

q) **Miscellaneous:** This is for small expenditures for which you don't have a separate category.

r) **Subtotal:** This figure is the sum of all the previous expenses and reflects the cash paid out for operating costs.

s) **Loan Principal Payment:** Record the principal portion of payments for all loans.

t) **Capital Purchases:** Expenditures that can be depreciated, e.g., equipment, vehicle purchases, computer purchases, leasehold improvements.

u) **Other Start-Up Costs:** Unless you are part of a start-up business that incurred expenses before the first month of operation, but paid for them afterward, you won't need to worry about this category.

v) **Reserve and/or Escrow:** Money that is set aside to reduce the impact of large payments that are made periodically, e.g., insurance or tax.

w) **Owner's Withdrawal:** This is money the owner takes out of the business for personal use and includes payment for items like life insurance premiums for executives.

To determine Calley Construction's cash position at the end of the month, subtract item 6, total cash paid out, from item 4, total cash available (see Figure 19). Do you remember where this figure shows up in the next month? Yes, as we discussed earlier, it becomes item 1, cash on hand, for the following month.

The last part of the cash flow statement provides essential operating data (non-cash flow information—see Figure 20). This is used mainly for planning and projecting cash flow. In the Calley Construction example, sales volume is broken down by product or service category.

3

ESSENTIAL OPERATING DATA				
(Non-cash flow information)				
A. Sales Volume (dollars)	22,691	26,639	30,321	79,651
by Product Category				
1) Earth work	10,370	11,417	12,911	34,698
2) Foundation work	12,321	15,222	17,410	44,953
B. Accounts Receivable (end of month)				
C. Bad Debt (end of month)				
D. Inventory on Hand (end of month)				
E. Accounts Payable (end of month)				
F. Depreciation				

Figure 20

Cash flow can be useful in a number of situations. Think back to the Laddie's Bookstore example in the previous chapter. If 60 percent of their business were generated through special orders that took two to three weeks, cash flow would become a major concern. Suppose that all special orders they place had to be paid on receipt. They could quickly be in trouble from a cash flow perspective if customers were not required to pay up front. Even if the store owner had 30 days to pay his account after receipt of the order, he would still have to consider having his customers pay up front or at least put down a deposit, since there is no guarantee they would come in to pay for their books in a timely manner once the books arrived.

Keep in mind that the cash flow statement gives you a history of where cash has typically gone, as well as a projection of where cash may go in the future. If you monitor cash flow regularly, you will probably start to see patterns.

Chapter Summary

The *cash flow statement* shows you where the cash in the business is going. *Cash flow* refers to the amount of cash you have available at a given point in time. It is usually figured on a month-by-month basis. Often, companies will juxtapose their actual results with their projections on the cash flow statement so that they can use the statement as a gauge.

A cash flow statement starts with the cash you had available at the beginning of the month and adds any money you received throughout the month to determine total cash available. From this, subtract the cash paid out to keep the business going. The result is the amount of cash on hand that you will have for the next month. This amount subtracted from your original amount is your cash flow.

Self-Check: Chapter 3 Review

Refer to the Calley Construction cash flow statement in Figure 15 to answer these questions. Answers are on page 90.

1. What is Calley Construction's cash position for the month of June?

   _____

2. What are the total cash receipts taken in for the month of May? Does this include jobs completed but not yet paid for by customers?

   _____

3. What were the total expenses for April?

   _____

4. What kinds of events might have an impact, positive or negative, on the cash flow?

   _____

3

Chapter *Four*

Using Financial Information

Chapter Objectives

▶ Determine ways to use the financial tools to analyze how well the business is doing.

▶ Forecast for the future and use that information as a management tool.

As a manager, you can use financial information in a variety of ways. Perhaps your department is hoping to introduce a new product. Which tool would give you the information you need to determine the best time to introduce the product from a financial standpoint?

_____

If you answered the cash flow statement, you're on the right track. This is the tool that shows you month by month where the cash is going.

What if you wanted to look at financial trends? For example, which tool would you use if you wanted to see how much the business is worth to the owners or stockholders this year as compared to last year?

_____

Yes, the balance sheet is the right answer. It allows you to look at net worth or owner's equity.

And finally, if you wanted to see how much profit the company achieved in a particular quarter, where would you look?

_____

Of course, the income statement, or P&L.

These are superficial analyses, but you can look deeper.

How Can I Tell How Well We Are Doing?

Before you can decide how to improve the future performance of your organization, department, or team, you need a clear picture of your current performance. Financial performance is one of the primary factors you need to consider. A common way to delve into financial performance is by using ratio analysis. The idea of working with ratios may seem a little foreboding, but like every aspect of financial management, the key lies in understanding some basic concepts.

Ratios are actually fairly simple. A ratio compares two numbers. In financial management, the numbers come from our three financial tools: the balance sheet, the income statement, and the cash flow statement. Although some standard ratios exist and are used regularly, you can find or create the ratios that make the most sense for your organization or department.

Checking Performance with Ratios

Figuring the Current Ratio

To help simplify the idea of ratios, let's start with an example from your childhood. Imagine that hot July afternoon when, as a young entrepreneur, you decide to set up a lemonade stand. You go to the corner store with money you borrowed from your older brother and invest $20 in a thermal jug, paper cups, sugar, lemons, poster board, and a marker. You agree to pay your brother half the loan by the end of July and the other half at the end of the summer.

Assets		Liabilities	
Current Assets		**Current Liabilities**	
Cash	$15.00	Accounts Payable	
Supplies `	$ 3.00	Current Portion Due on Loan	$10.00
Total Current Assets	**$ 18.00**	**Total Current Liabilities**	$10.00
Fixed Assets		**Long-Term Liabilities**	
Thermal Jug	$12.00	Loan	$10.00
Sign	$ 2.00		
Stand	$ 5.00		
Total Fixed Assets	**$19.00**	**Total Long-Term Liabilities**	$20.00
Total Assets	**$37.00**	**Net Worth**	$17.00
		Total Liabilities & Net Worth	$37.00

Figure 21

You open up shop and immediately begin selling. At the end of the month, you are ready to give your brother $10 toward the money you owe him. Being a wise businessperson, you develop a balance sheet.

Note: For the purpose of example, consider the $20 loan as a long-term liability even though it does not meet the standard definition of a long-term liability. Also, remember that the fixed assets would probably be depreciated were this a real business.

As you examine your balance sheet, you wonder how your performance compares to that of other lemonade stands. What about the amount of money you owe on the stand—do you have a large amount of liabilities when compared to your assets? In talking with the owners of other lemonade stands, and particularly with your brother (who had one when he was young), you discover that by the end of previous summers, most of them have had $2 of current assets for every dollar of current liabilities. In business terms, this is known as a *current ratio* of 2:1 or 2. This ratio is determined by dividing the current assets by the current liabilities.

$$\text{Current Ratio} = \frac{\text{Current Assets}}{\text{Current Liabilities}}$$

So for the lemonade business, a ratio of 2:1 is the industry standard. To see how your lemonade stand is doing compared to that standard, figure your own ratios by comparing your current assets to your current liabilities. In the July balance sheet shown on the previous page, your current assets are $18. To create the ratio, divide $18 by your current liabilities, or $10. Your current ratio, then, is 1.8. This means that for every dollar of liability, you have $1.80 in current assets. If you know that the industry standard is $2 for every $1, you can see that you have room for improvement if you are going to compete with other lemonade stands.

You might also use the current ratio to see how much you are improving over the summer. At the end of August, your balance sheet looks like this (Figure 22):

4

Pucker-Up Lemonade
August 31

Assets		Liabilities	
Current Assets		**Current Liabilities**	
Cash	$25.00	Accounts Payable	
Supplies	$ 2.00	Current Portion	
		Due on Loan	$10.00
Total Current		**Total Current Liabilities**	$10.00
Assets	$27.00		
Fixed Assets		**Long-Term Liabilities**	
Thermal Jug	$12.00	Loan	
Sign	$ 2.00		
Stand	$ 5.00		
Total Fixed Assets	$19.00	**Total Long-Term Liabilities**	$10.00
Total Assets	$46.00	**Net Worth**	$36.00
		Total Liabilities &	
		Net Worth	$46.00

Figure 22

Now the current ratio is based on $27 in current assets divided by $10 in current liabilities. Your current ratio at the end of August is 2.7, or $2.70 of current assets for every $1 of current liability. Now that your company has a history, you can use these figures to compare on three levels:

◆ Your present performance compared with past performance

◆ Your performance compared with the performance of other companies

◆ Your performance compared with standard performance for your industry

First, you can compare your current ratio at the end of July to your current ratio at the end of August. By doing this, you can see that you have improved vastly. If you have balance sheets from your brother's lemonade stand when he was young, you can see how your business compares to his—especially useful because you're operating from the same location.

Finally, you can see that you are doing better than the industry standard, which has a current ratio of 2 or $2 in current assets for every dollar of current liability.

Take a Moment

Use the balance sheet for Calley Construction to answer the following questions. Selected answers appear on page 90.

1. How much are Calley Construction's total current assets?

   _____

2. How much are the total current liabilities?

   _____

3. Calculate the current ratio.

   _____

4. How could the owner use this current ratio?

   _____

Calley Construction
July 1
Balance Sheet

Assets			Liabilities		
Current Assets			**Current Liabilities**		
Cash	$3,500		Accounts payable	$4,000	
Petty cash	$500		Current portion due on notes/loan	$1,000	
Accounts receivable	$10,000		Payroll	$3,600	
Supplies	$5,000		Taxes payable	$5,000	
Prepaid expenses	$2,500		**Total Current Liabilities**		$13,600
Total Current Assets		$ 21,500	**Long-Term Liabilities**		
Fixed Assets			Bank loan	$100,000	
Office furniture	$4,000		Vehicle loan	$4,000	
Office equipment	$10,000		**Total Long-Term Liabilities**		$104,000
Construction equipment	$150,000				
Vehicles	$32,000				
Total Fixed Assets	$196,000				
Less Accumulated Depreciation	$25,000				
Net Fixed Assets		$171,000	**Total Liabilities**		$117,600
Other Assets		$0	**Net Worth or Owner's Equity**	$74,900	
Total Assets		$192,500	**Total Liabilities and Net Worth**		$192,500

4

The current ratio is largely a gauge for your daily operations—
especially if you have a great deal of long-term liability and a
substantial number of fixed assets. There are, however, many aspects
of your business's performance that a current ratio will not reveal.
To illustrate, let's return to our lemonade stand example.

57

The current ratios we figured for your lemonade stand told us how the business was doing, but they did not tell us why the business was performing this way. The second current ratio of 2.7 was very encouraging, but what if your improved performance is due to the fact that your mother donated the sugar and lemons to replenish your supplies for the second month? A person interested in buying your business would have no way of knowing this if he or she looked only at the current ratio. As this example illustrates, the current ratio is most effective in providing a starting point for diagnosing your company's problems or determining why your business is healthy, but it cannot provide a thorough explanation for your performance.

Liquidity ratios help you determine how liquid a business is and, consequently, how well that business can meet short-term obligations.

The current ratio belongs to a category of ratios called *liquidity ratios.* Liquidity ratios help you determine how liquid a business is and, consequently, how well that business can meet short-term obligations. Liquidity ratios are especially useful if you are contemplating the purchase of another business because they can give you a quick figure for evaluation. Another commonly used liquidity ratio is the *quick ratio.* The quick ratio is figured like the current ratio, but it considers not only the current assets, but also securities that can quickly be turned into cash and receivables. Both the current ratio and the quick ratio lend insight into the company's likelihood of remaining solvent.

Figuring the Profitability Ratio

Another useful ratio is the profitability ratio. Although you most often look at net income from the income statement or the cash flow statement as a gauge of profitability, using a ratio to compare two numbers can give you a more accurate picture. Profitability ratios can help you see how effectively you invest money and build sales to get a return on that money. This is your *return on investment,* or ROI. The following is the formula for a profitability ratio:

$$ROI = \frac{\text{Net profit}}{\text{Total assets}}$$

As net profits increase, so does the return on investment, as you can see in the following exercise.

Take a Moment

Look at Calley Construction's income statement and calculate the return on investment using the profitability ratio. Total assets as of June 30 were $192,500. Selected answers appear on page 90.

4

Calley Construction
Income Statement
for the Quarter Ending June 30

Earth Work	$ 40,015
Foundation Work	$ 67,005
Sales/Revenue	$107,020
Cost of Goods Sold	
Direct Labor	$ 65,000
Material	$ 8,987
Gross Profit	$ 33,033
Operating Expenses	
Selling Expenses	$ 300
Salaries	$ 6,800
Advertising	$ 300
Other	$ 200
General Administrative	$ 300
Depreciation	$ 6,250
Total Operating Expenses	$ 14,150
Income from Operations	
(Gross profit—total	
operating expenses)	$ 18,883
Interest Expense	$ 800
Interest Income	$ 0
Income Before Taxes	$ 18,003
Income Taxes	$ 6,301
Net Income After Taxes	$ 11,702
Net Increase (or Decrease)	
to Retained Earnings	$_____

Suppose that Calley had a net profit of $20,312. What happens to the return on investment?

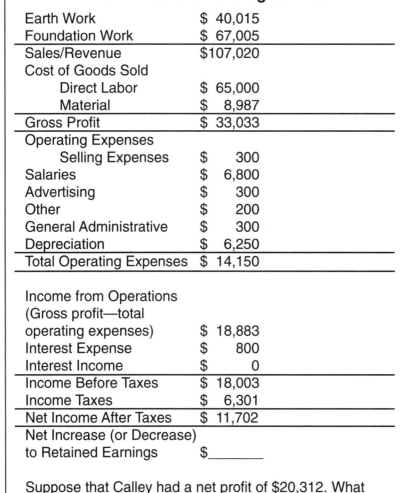

Figuring Efficiency Ratios

Efficiency ratios help you look at how well the company handles items like inventory and accounts receivable. Managers in retail businesses will find the *inventory turnover ratio* useful. It compares the cost of goods sold with the average inventory balance. Similarly, managers in service businesses use *accounts receivable ratios* related to the time it takes to collect receivables—a shorter collection period means a better cash flow. Both of these ratios tell managers something about cash flow, as well as their use of funds. In short, ratios highlight what you are doing well and what you are doing poorly.

Efficiency ratios help you look at how well the company handles items like inventory and accounts receivable.

The following demonstrates a situation in which an efficiency ratio is useful:

■ Yoshi owns an engine-repair business. She knows that sales have increased over the past year; however, her cash flow is a problem. For the past few months, the company has had barely enough cash to pay its bills. This was not the case a year ago when sales were lower. In order to diagnose her cash flow problem, Yoshi decides to look at receivable turnover. The receivable turnover ratio can show Yoshi how many times, on the average, accounts receivable were turned into cash for a designated period. Yoshi decides to look at the first quarter of this year compared to the same quarter last year. Using data from the balance sheet and the income statement, Yoshi divides sales by accounts receivable.

Year 1
$32,000 in sales
$ 3,500 accounts receivable = 9.1

Year 2
$36,000 in sales
$ 5,000 accounts receivables = 7.2

Yoshi discovers that in the first quarter of Year 1, she converted her cash into receivables 9.1 times, whereas in Year 2, she did so only 7.2 times. Consequently, even though her sales had increased in Year 2, she had less cash with which to work.

Yoshi then goes a step further in her diagnosis by figuring out how many days, on the average, sales went uncollected. This is especially useful because her credit terms are stated to customers in days. She uses the following ratio to do this:

$$\frac{\text{Days in the year}}{\text{Receivable turnover}}$$

To calculate the ratio for Year 1, Yoshi divides 365 (the number of days in a year) by 9.1 (receivable turnover) for a total of 40.1 days. To calculate the ratio for Year 2, she divides 365 by 7.2 for a total of 50.7 days.

As the ratios illustrate, Yoshi has been waiting far longer in Year 2 to collect receivables from her customers than she did in Year 1. Once Yoshi looks at this information, she can review her credit policy, think about what is in her control and what is not, and develop a strategy for improvement.

Choose the Ratio That's Right for You

Remember: Regardless of the measures you use, do what makes sense for your organization or department. For example, if you work for a large company, you probably will not develop a separate balance sheet for your department. Consequently, the current ratio may not be the most useful to you. Figure out what you need to measure and work with the accounting or finance department to develop the tools that will help you do it, even if those tools are unique to your industry.

No magic formula exists that says one particular ratio is the most effective one to use and another one is the least effective. Calley Construction may want to look at a ratio that compares expenses for equipment repair with sales. Consider this scenario: For the first four months of the year, repair costs are negligible. Then in May, a major part on an important piece of equipment breaks and the machine is down for a week. Fortunately, the manager is able to rent another so that production can continue. By using a ratio, the manager can compare the repair expense per dollar of sales for May to an average repair cost. Another measure could compare repair ratios for two different pieces of the same type of equipment, one new and another older. The manager could then do a cost-benefit analysis of buying equipment versus maintaining the existing equipment.

Regardless of the measure you decide to use, don't get mired in short-term concerns at the expense of long-term returns. For example, investing in equipment may create higher debt and lower net income, which will be reflected on the income statement and the cash flow. The return on that investment may be realized down the road and may well be worth the short-term pain.

To use ratios most effectively, decide what is most important to you. Do you need to focus on profitability by customer, department, or product? Maybe you will want to compare labor costs to net income. It doesn't matter, as long as it makes sense and is meaningful to your business.

Using Future Projections to Create a Budget

A *budget* is a plan that allows a manager to set goals based on financial figures and measure performance against those figures.

As a manager, you may be asked to forecast costs for the following year so you can develop a budget. An effective forecast is based on the financial information found in the tools we have discussed: the balance sheet, the income statement, and the cash flow statement.

A *budget* is a plan that allows a manager to do two things:

♦ Set goals based on financial figures.

♦ Follow up by measuring actual performance against those figures.

Managers can use the budget as a communication tool for discussing performance with their departments and teams. In large companies, a budget can also serve as a source of financial coordination across the company.

The first step in creating a budget is to look at external issues. These can include:

♦ Industry trends.

♦ Changes in your customer base.

♦ New technology.

For the manager of a specific department, external issues may actually be internal to the company. For example, if you are in production, sales volume may be an external issue with which you need to be concerned. If the sales department projects an increase in sales, that will have an impact on your budget. This illustrates why communication across organizational departments is vital for budgetary planning.

The second step in creating a budget is to forecast costs for the next operating period. In doing this, you must establish basic assumptions you will use as you develop your budget. For example, you may know that you need to borrow money, but you may not know for sure what the interest rate will be. Your projections will be based on an assumption, for example, that you will borrow the money at 10 percent interest for six years.

> To create a budget, you will need to consider external issues and forecast costs for the next operating period.

4

Forecasting Costs with Pro Forma Financial Statements

You may find *pro forma financial statements* helpful for projecting future costs and income. (*Pro forma* is a Latin term meaning something that's provided in advance to describe items.) Pro forma financial statements are based on the three financial tools we have discussed so far:

◆ The *pro forma balance sheet* can help you see what your cash position will be at the end of the next operating period. This can be especially helpful if you are managing a small company. If the projections show the company to be short of cash, you know you will need to borrow funds.

◆ The *pro forma income statement* is a projection of what the income will be over the next operating period. This helps you budget for the next operating period so that you can make intelligent financial decisions (see Figure 23).

Pro Forma Income Statement

| Where We Are | Balance Sheet | ●●●●●●► | Pro forma Balance Sheet | Where We Expect to Be |

Figure 23

What we expect will happen in the interim

◆ The *pro forma cash flow statement* helps you see if you can survive financially, even if you know the business is viable from a profit standpoint.

To see how financial projections work, let's consider the following scenario:

■ A large mortgage company headquartered in Colorado wants to expand to a metropolitan area in the eastern United States. Management has done enough research to know that the market is viable. They found that new home development in this metropolitan area is booming and that several small mortgage companies were recently swallowed up by a large financial conglomerate whose reputation is less than favorable. Additionally, the Colorado company is one of the only mortgage companies with a well-defined strategy for reaching Hispanic customers, a growing population in the targeted metropolitan area. Clearly, the business potential is there.

Within this scenario, sales will increase, adding a projected $500,000 to the cash flow and ultimately to the balance sheet in the first six months. More money coming into the company is always a good thing, but can the company do it with their existing resources? Probably not. So what will it take to increase the sales in the new market? Consider the following:

◆ Additional labor costs to hire people to bring in these sales

◆ Training for the new people

◆ Expenses for office space and computer equipment

◆ Additional costs for marketing and advertising in order to penetrate the new market

The projected total of these additional costs is $800,000.

The additional costs will show up on the financial statements and will have a definite impact on the cash flow. If management figures in the $500,000 worth of sales they project for the first six months but forgets to account for the $800,000 worth of expenses necessary to move into the new market, they will have skewed financial projections, making it impossible to tell whether the division could survive on its own for the first year.

Take a Moment

Calley Construction has spent the past six months building a good working relationship with a land development company. This company recently purchased a 50-acre plot of land on which it will develop new homes. It has offered Calley Construction a contract to do the earth and foundation work. These homes will be well above the median cost per home in the area, and the lots will be sold off at an acre per home. This information can be used to help forecast sales for the next operating period.

Increasing income usually decreases funds in the short term but increases funds in the long term. This will probably be the case with Calley Construction. If they intend to continue working with existing clients as well as with their new client, they need to make a financial forecast. List some of the issues the company should consider (author's suggestions appear on page 91):

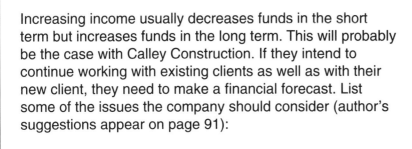

The pro forma income statement and balance sheet can help Calley Construction project their overall financial status if they take on this project. Particularly, the pro forma income statement will help them assess increased sales and increased expenses to see if this is a profitable venture. A projected cash flow will help them see if they can get by month to month and cover expenses.

4

Once the pro forma cash flow analysis is done, you can use it for planning. If you see via the income statement that the activities for the next period are viable in terms of profitability, but not viable in terms of cash flow, you have several options besides abandoning your plans. You can increase your cash by:

◆ Collecting the money due the company (accounts receivable).

◆ Requiring customers to pay cash rather than extending credit.

◆ Changing the price of the product or service.

◆ Securing a loan.

◆ Increasing sales.

The glory of financial forecasting is to be able to do "what if?" scenarios as a way to plan for the future. This is especially true when you have a computer and software that allows you to plug in different numbers to see the impact they have in different scenarios. You can work with your accounting and finance department to customize software to do that or sit down with your favorite spreadsheet and create it yourself.

The Importance of Flexibility

A budget is a target you aim for, but not at the cost of quality, customer service, or some other element that is essential to the mission of your company.

One of the dangers of creating a budget in some companies is that it often becomes rigid. Budgeting and forecasting should be ongoing, flexible processes. A budget is a target you aim for, but not at the cost of quality, customer service, or some other element that is essential to the mission of your company. The figures you use in forecasting are indeed guesses, but if done correctly, they are calculated, intelligent guesses. If you include your department or team in the process of forecasting and budgeting, the collective effort will probably make those figures more accurate and will offer other benefits: You won't bear the entire burden (or opportunity) alone, and you can encourage ownership for the results by enlisting help.

Chapter Summary

The most important point to remember when working with financial reports is to identify and use the tools that best meet your needs. Don't feel obligated to use every financial report you receive or every tool that was discussed in this chapter.

Ratio analysis, especially when customized for your part of the business, is an effective way to make comparisons. Ratios compare two numbers, both of which will come from one of the three financial tools: the balance sheet, the income statement, or the cash flow statement. Use ratios to make comparisons on three levels:

◆ Compare your present performance with your past performance.

◆ Compare your performance with the performance of specific other companies.

◆ Compare your performance with an industry standard.

Like ratios, an effective budget will be based on the three financial tools. Look at the big picture by thinking about industry trends, changes in your customer base, and new technology before you use pro forma financial statements to project your future costs and income. Building a budget for your department or team allows you to do two things:

◆ Set goals.

◆ Track performance by measuring actual performance against the figures you forecast for the budget.

Intelligent decision making hinges on intelligent planning.

4

Self-Check: Chapter 4 Review

Answers appear on page 91.

1. If your company were considering the purchase of another business, what is one type of ratio you might use to compare their business results to yours?

   _____

2. What happens to a company's return on investment (ROI) if their net profits increase while their assets stay the same? Is this good or bad?

   _____

   _____

3. What is a *pro forma financial statement?*

   _____

   _____

4. If you do a pro forma cash flow analysis and discover that the activities for the next time period are not realistic, what are two steps you might take in your planning?

   a. _____

   b. _____

5. List three ideas for tools that might be useful in your tracking and planning efforts.

   a. _____

   b. _____

   c. _____

Chapter *Five*

Building Ownership with Meaningful Financial Data

Chapter Objectives

▶ Identify your objective for sharing financial information with employees.

▶ Determine what information to share with employees.

▶ Communicate effectively to make that information meaningful to employees.

▶ Encourage employee feedback regarding financial information.

▶ Support employee ownership of financial goals.

> Often, managers aren't sure how to present financial information to others, especially their own employees.

We have seen a number of ways in which you can use financial information to follow and predict the performance of your organization, department, or team. How should you share this information? Often, managers aren't sure how to present financial information to others, especially their own employees. Some managers will put a financial report on an overhead projector during a meeting without really thinking about the reasons for doing so or whether employees will understand the information. Employees may try to clarify the information by asking questions—or they may just look at it in silence.

Take a Moment

Describe the worst experience you have had in which someone shared financial information with you.

_____

_____

_____

Now think about the worst experience you have had sharing financial information with others. Did people seem confused? Did they ask questions? Or was there no response at all?

_____

_____

_____

If employees are greeting your financial information with silence, perhaps they simply don't know what to ask. Consider the following example:

■ Berta worked for a Fortune 500 company that was establishing work teams. To help the teams become more accountable for financial decisions, management began sharing financial information with employees. Berta wanted to understand the information, but to her, every financial report looked like it was written in a foreign language. She wanted to ask questions, but she was so confused, she didn't even know what questions to ask. The result was that she had no idea what she was supposed to look for in the data, let alone how she could have an impact on it.

> **If employees are greeting your financial information with silence, perhaps they simply don't know what to ask.**

5

Steps for Effectively Sharing Financial Information

To avoid confusing your employees in this way, follow these guidelines for sharing financial information:

1. Determine *why* you are sharing the information. What is your objective?

2. Decide *what* information will help you meet that objective.

3 Be sure that *you* understand the information before you present it.

4. *Present* the information in a way employees can understand.

5. Encourage employee *feedback.*

6. Use financial information to help employees *take ownership* of your organization's financial goals.

Step 1: Determine Why You Are Sharing the Information

Before you present financial information to employees, ask yourself *why* you want to share it. Your objective for sharing that information will help you determine what information to share and how to present it.

There are many reasons for sharing financial information. One very good reason is to help your team meet its own departmental or organizational performance goals—or ideally, to help set them. There are many other reasons as well. Perhaps you are concerned about the financial impact of production errors, supply costs, or employee turnover. Or you might want your team to recognize the effect—positive or negative—that their performance has on the organization as a whole. Sharing financial information can help employees see the full impact of these and other important issues.

> **Before you present financial information to employees, ask yourself *why* you want to share it.**

Take a Moment

List some reasons why you might share financial
information with your employees.

_____

_____

_____

_____

Step 2: Decide What Information Will Help You Meet Your Objective

Your objectives for sharing information will help you determine
what information to share. Remember that you do not want to
overload your employees with too much financial information.
Instead, try to determine *what* information will be relevant to
them and to the objective you hope to accomplish.

5

Determine
what informa-
tion will be
relevant to
employees and
to the objective
you hope to
accomplish.

◆ If you want employees to understand the overall financial
health of the organization, show them data from the balance
sheet. A bar chart showing quarterly comparisons of the
current year and the previous year would clearly
communicate that information.

◆ If you want employees to understand how your department
contributes to the overall financial health of the
organization, compare the balance sheet for the entire
company with a balance sheet that you create for your
department. Another approach would be to use the
company's income statement to show employees what
percent of the overall income your department generates and
how departmental expenses compare to overall
organizational expenses.

◆ If you want employees to recognize the impact of specific
aspects of your operations, such as production errors, supply
costs, or employee turnover, show them some ratios that
reflect these issues.

♦ If you want employees to help set performance and financial goals for your department, show them any of the reports mentioned on the previous page. Ratios can be especially useful in setting goals. For example, if you have determined that for every 10 widgets the department creates, three are rejected because of quality, set a goal and put a plan in place for reducing that number. Use the budget as well as pro forma financial statements to help the department determine how they will have to improve.

Each of these objectives varies in terms of anticipated outcomes. Creating an understanding or an awareness requires a different approach from creating action plans and goals. Know your purpose and choose the information accordingly.

Take a Moment

Can you identify the types of financial information that would be most useful to your employees based on the objectives you listed in the Take a Moment exercise on page 73? List them below.

_____

_____

_____

_____

Step 3: Be Sure That *You* Understand the Information

Never share financial information with employees unless *you* fully understand it yourself.

Never share financial information with employees unless *you* fully understand it yourself. Full understanding means more than just being able to read numbers off a balance sheet. Your employees may have questions about the material you present— are you prepared to answer them? Try to anticipate the types of questions employees may ask and research possible answers beforehand. If you are insecure about your own ability to answer financial questions, ask a member of the accounting or finance department to help you prepare. You might even ask that person to attend your presentation to help you answer questions and address employee concerns.

Step 4: Present the Information in a Way Employees Can Understand

How should you present financial information to your employees? As with any communication situation, you will need to consider the needs and prior experience of your audience. If you have a team or department that is well versed in finance and knows how to use financial information to set goals and evaluate progress, sending a memo or posting financial information on a bulletin board or computer scoreboard may be all that is necessary. If you have a group who understands financial information but has no motivation to deal with it, small-group meetings may be more appropriate. And if you have a group who doesn't even know enough about finance to ask questions, combine information sharing with training and be careful not to overwhelm them with too much information at once.

> Consider the needs and prior experience of your audience.

If you have a diverse group, consider using more than one method to share financial information. While one employee may have an affinity for numbers and learn easily in a large group, another may have anxiety about numbers and need the personal interaction offered in a small-group setting. Whatever methods you use, make sure that the information you present is simple and easy to understand.

5

Presentation Tips

If you decide to make an oral presentation in either a large- or small-group setting, following these guidelines will make your presentation more effective:

◆ **Choose an appropriate time.** Schedule your presentation for a date and time when people will be able to give your information their full attention. Avoid scheduling a presentation late in the day when people are tired and ready to go home. If your department or team is feeling pressured because of a tight deadline, don't create more stress by insisting that they sit through a financial presentation—save your information for a calmer day.

◆ **Support your presentation with visual aids.** Research shows that audience members understand and retain more information when an oral presentation is supported with visual aids. To illustrate, consider the following example: What would your reaction be to an overhead transparency showing two balance sheets side by side versus this chart representing the same information?

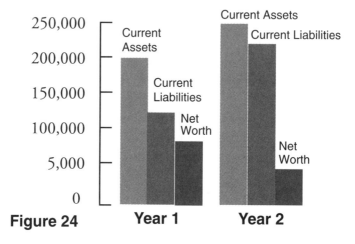

Figure 24

More than likely, you would find the bar chart easier to understand because it would allow you to quickly focus on specific information.

Visual aids do not need to be fancy. You can provide audience members with handouts, write figures on a flip chart or whiteboard, or present material on an overhead projector. Whatever style of visual aid you choose, be sure that your aids are legible and that they are well integrated into your spoken message. Never present audience members with a visual aid without thoroughly explaining the information it conveys.

You don't have to be a polished speaker to present financial information effectively, but your audience does have to be able to hear and understand you.

◆ **Practice effective delivery skills.** You don't have to be a polished speaker to present financial information effectively, but your audience does have to be able to hear and understand you. Adjust your voice volume to the size of the room—if you aren't sure whether you're speaking loudly enough, ask the people in the back whether they can hear you. Many people find that they speak more quickly when they are excited or nervous. Slow down your rate of speech so you can enunciate clearly. If you are reading from notes, be sure to look up regularly and make eye contact with your audience.

◆ **Select an appropriate environment.** Choose an environment that is as conducive to your presentation as possible. A conference room or some other type of meeting space in which your audience can sit comfortably is ideal. If your organization doesn't have this type of facility, try to find an area in which you can address employees without being interrupted by outside distractions. Try to avoid as many environmental distractions as possible: Be sure that the room is a comfortable temperature and that the lighting is adequate. If you are planning to use a flip chart, whiteboard, or overhead transparencies, be sure that the room has the appropriate facilities. (If it doesn't, you may need to change the format of your visual aids.)

Step 5: Encourage Employee Feedback

Effective communication is two-way communication. Don't just present your employees with financial information—ask for their feedback on that information. You can begin by asking for feedback on your presentation itself. Some questions you might ask include:

Don't just present your employees with financial information— ask for their feedback on that information.

5

◆ Did employees find the format you used to present the information effective?

◆ Would they have liked the information presented in some other way? If so, how?

◆ Do they fully understand all the information you discussed with them? Would they like anything explained further?

◆ Are they receiving all the information they need to make financial decisions?

◆ What other suggestions do they have for making financial information accessible?

Besides asking employees for feedback on how financial information is presented, you should also ask for their reactions to the information they receive. Some questions of this nature include:

◆ What goals should your department set to play a full role in meeting the overall goals of the organization?

◆ How does your department's current performance measure up to its goals?

◆ What are the strongest aspects of your department's financial performance? What aspects of your department's financial performance could use improvement?

Encouraging your employees to discuss financial information in this way is the first step toward helping them take ownership of your organization's financial goals.

Step 6: Help Employees Take Ownership of Financial Goals

If the financial information you present is clear and meaningful, employees should start to see how their performance affects it.

If it seems appropriate, you can gradually shift the responsibility of reporting financial information and setting financial goals to the members of your team or department. As team members take over more and more of this responsibility, you can take on the role of coach as you help them continue to improve their financial skills.

If you work in an organization in which it is not feasible to give employees full ownership of financial goals, focus on helping them see the financial impact of their daily actions. If the financial information you present is clear and meaningful, employees should start to see how their performance affects it. When employees recognize each of them is responsible for your organization's financial health, they move from merely participating in the business to taking responsibility for its success.

Chapter Summary

Many managers who understand financial management themselves are confused about how to share that information with employees. The following steps will help you share information with employees in a way that they can understand:

1. **Determine *why* you are sharing the information.**
    What is your objective? Managers often share financial information as a way to help employees own departmental or organizational performance goals or to help set them.

2. **Decide *what* information will help you meet that objective.**
    Your objective for sharing information will help you determine what information to share. Sharing only relevant information will also help keep you from overloading your employees with more information than they can use.

3. **Be sure that *you* understand the information before you present it.**
    Don't share information unless you are comfortable discussing it and answering questions. If you need help with your presentation, talk to someone in your accounting or finance department.

4. ***Present* the information in a way that employees can understand.**
    Adapt your presentation to your audience's needs. An audience skilled in financial management might need only a brief memo or figures posted on a bulletin board; an audience with fewer financial skills would need training as well as information sharing.

5. **Encourage employee *feedback*.**
    Ask employees for their reactions to your presentation as well as to the financial information itself.

6. **Use financial information to help employees *take ownership* of your organization's financial goals.**
    If appropriate, you can hand over responsibility of reporting financial information and setting financial goals to members of your team or department.

5

Self-Check: Chapter 5 Review

Answers for these questions appear on page 91.

1. What is likely to happen if you present financial information that you don't understand?

   _____

   _____

2. What are some alternative methods of information sharing besides the traditional meeting where you present the information to employees?

   _____

   _____

   _____

3. What information would you use to determine the appropriate method?

   _____

   _____

4. List two or three ideas you might use to share financial information with your team or department.

   _____

   _____

   _____

5. Write down an idea for enlisting your team or department's help in tracking financial performance in the future.

   _____

   _____

Final Assessment

Take the following assessment to measure your knowledge of basic finance. You may check more than one answer for multiple-choice questions. Answers appear at the end of the assessment.

1. Another term for the P&L, or profit and loss statement, is
   a. Balance sheet
   b. Income statement
   c. Ratio analysis statement
   d. Cash flow statement

2. If you work for a large company that has an accounting department, in which one of the following steps are you most likely to play a role?
   a. Integrating information into financial records
   b. Creating financial reports
   c. Taking action and making decisions based on financial reports
   d. Recording information, such as cost of goods, sales information, or hours worked

3. The balance sheet helps you see the following:
   a. Assets and profit
   b. Liabilities and cost of goods sold
   c. Assets and liabilities
   d. Cash flow and current ratio

4. The most effective ratio to use if you are considering the purchase of another business is the
   a. Accounts receivable ratio
   b. Inventory turnover ratio
   c. Current ratio
   d. Return on investment ratio

5. Which of the following are considered liabilities?
   a. Inventory
   b. Bank loans
   c. Payroll
   d. Accounts receivable

6. If the balance sheet shows the total assets to be $150,000 and the total liabilities to be $115,000, then net worth would be
   a. $265,000
   b. -$35,000
   c. $35,000
   d. $0

7. The following items are considered fixed assets:
   a. Petty cash
   b. Production equipment
   c. Computers
   d. Supplies

8. Depreciation for a piece of equipment is calculated in the following way:
   a. By dividing a piece of equipment's value by the amount of your fixed assets
   b. By adding 10 percent to the original purchase price
   c. By comparing the cost of a used piece of equipment to the price of a new piece of equipment
   d. By using an IRS schedule to determine the value

9. The profit and loss statement serves the following purpose:
   a. It gives you a picture of what happened financially over a period of time.
   b. It gives you a snapshot of a specific point in time.
   c. It shows you when you will need cash and for what purposes.
   d. It allows you to compare your assets and liabilities.

10. Which of these are key elements that make up the profit and loss statement?
   a. Interest expenses
   b. Cost of goods sold
   c. Sales/revenue
   d. Operating expenses

11. The profit and loss statement compares
   a. Sales and revenue to net income
   b. Sales and revenue to expenses
   c. Sales and revenue to inventory turnover
   d. Sales and revenue to capital purchases

12. The cash flow statement deals with cash income and expenditures by showing
    a. How much money the business has
    b. When the business needs that money
    c. Where the business will get its money
    d. How much net worth is in the business

13. List the three items you need in order to prepare a cash flow statement.

    a. _____

    b. _____

    c. _____

14. What is the basic formula for calculating cash flow?

    _____

    _____

15. What are the three financial tools you will use to create ratios?

    a. _____

    b. _____

    c. _____

16. Managers can use ratios to compare information on three levels:
    a. Present performance compared with past performance
    b. Your organization's performance compared with the performance of other companies
    c. _____

17. Which ratio will help you see how effectively you invest money and build sales to get a return on your money?

    _____

18. Which ratio will help you evaluate how many times receivables are turned into cash for a particular period of time?

    _____

19. True or False?
    You should create a ratio that makes the most sense for your department or company.

20. True or False?
    A pro forma financial statement helps you look at financial records from previous years.

21. True or False?
    If a cash flow analysis shows that activities for the next period are not viable in terms of cash flow even though they are viable in terms of profitability, there is little you can do to be successful.

22. True or False?
    A budget can help your department or team set goals and track performance effectively.

23. What should be your first step in sharing financial information?

    _____

24. List three ways you might share financial information.

    a. _____

    b. _____

    c. _____

25. List two advantages of understanding the basics of financial management.

    a. _____

    b. _____

Answers to Final Assessment

1. b. Income statement (page 26)

2. c. Taking action and making decisions based on financial reports (page 8)

3. c. Assets and liabilities (page 16)

4. c. Current ratio (page 53)

5. b. Bank loans
   c. Payroll (page 23)

6. c. $35,000 (page 25)

7. b. Production equipment
   c. Computers (page 19)

8. d. By using an IRS schedule to determine the value (page 21)

9. a. It gives you a picture of what happened financially over a period of time. (page 26)

10. a. Interest expenses
    b. Cost of goods sold
    c. Sales/revenue
    d. Operating expenses (page 27)

11. b. Sales and revenue to expenses (page 28)

12. a. How much money the business has
    b. When the business needs that money
    c. Where the business will get its money (page 38)

13. a. Cash available at the beginning of the month
    b. Cash receipts/sales figures (amount you sold)
    c. The amount spent (page 41)

14. Cash available at the beginning of the month + Money received throughout the month - Money paid out to cover business expenses (page 41)

15. a. Balance sheet
    b. Income statement, or profit and loss statement
    c. Cash flow statement (page 53)

16. c. Your organization's performance compared with the standard performance for the industry (page 56)

17. Return on investment (ROI) ratio (page 58)

18. Accounts receivable ratio (page 60)

19. True—You should create a ratio that makes the most sense for your department or company. (page 61)

20. False—A pro forma financial statement helps you project future costs and income. (page 63)

21. False—If a cash flow analysis shows that activities for the next period are not viable in terms of cash flow, you can collect accounts receivable, require customers to pay cash, change pricing, secure a loan, or increase sales. (page 66)

22. True—A budget can help your department or team set goals and track performance effectively. (page 62)

23. Determine your objective for sharing it (page 72)

24. Choose from:
    a. One on one
    b. In small groups
    c. In a formal presentation
    d. On a department bulletin board or a computer scoreboard (page 75)

25. a. It provides a basis for intelligent decision making.
    b. It can help you increase profits.
    c. It can be used as a tool for improvement (measurement).
    d. It builds ownership across the organization. (page 11)

Answers to Selected Exercises
Chapter 1
Take a Moment, page 10

1. She might plan to use tools that are too expensive. She could be asked to redo the project because of this.

2. The department could be eliminated.

3. By using effective financial management tools.

Chapter Review, page 14

1. All members of an organization are responsible for that organization's financial management.

2. a. It provides a basis for intelligent decision making.
   b. It can increase profits.
   c. It can be used as a tool for improvement (measurement).
   d. It builds ownership across the organization.

3. Step 1: You record information that affects the company's financial system.
   Step 2: The information is integrated into financial records.
   Step 3: Financial reports are created.
   Step 4: You take actions and make decisions based on the reports.

4. Answers will vary.

Chapter 2
Take a Moment, page 26

1. Current assets—cash and other assets that can easily be turned into cash.
   Fixed assets—permanent investments, usually necessary for the day-to-day operation of the business.

2. A bank loan, a loan for equipment, a mortgage.

3. Subtract the total liabilities from the total assets.

4. In construction equipment.

5. Computer equipment, machinery, vehicles—items that wear out.

Take a Moment, page 34

1. They spent more money than they took in. They made more money doing earth work than they did foundation work. (At first glance, you might have thought foundation work was the most profitable—look again. Foundation work had higher sales, but earth work had a higher profit.)

2. Bad weather conditions might have been a problem. Equipment might have broken down. They might have bought new equipment since they depreciated $6,250.

Chapter Review, page 36

1. Sales are determined by adding together the first two numbers on the income sheet. Sales in the first quarter amounted to $75,000.

2. The part-time person's wages are a direct labor cost associated with selling the books. You would find it as a subheading under cost of goods sold.

3. This too should go under cost of goods sold. In addition to the cost of inventory for used books, you would also find the cost of inventory for new books.

4. The cost of the newsletter would show up under advertising or selling costs, depending on how the newsletter is distributed and used. Either way, it would be an operating expense rather than figured as part of the cost of goods sold. The store could sell books whether they had the newsletter or not.

5. Income taxes go in the income taxes space. That was an easy answer—but it's important, because you don't want to forget about the taxes as you look at net income.

Chapter 3

Chapter Review, page 51

1. $35,469

2. $32,989—This figure does not include jobs completed but not yet paid for by customers.

3. $22,072

4. Many things could affect cash flow, including nonpayment of money owed to the company, unexpected expenses, such as repairs, and a drop in business.

Chapter 4

Take a Moment, page 56

1. $21,500

2. $13,600

3. Divide the current assets by the current liabilities to get the ratio 1.06.

4. The owners could use the ratio to compare their business to others. They could also use it to compare their current financial status to a previous or to an industry standard.

Take a Moment, page 59

Remember that the ROI equals the net profit divided by the total assets. In the first instance, $ROI = \dfrac{\$\ 11,702}{\$192,500}$
which leaves us with a ratio of 0.06.
In the second instance, $ROI = \dfrac{\$\ 20,312}{\$192,500}$
which leaves us with a ratio of 0.10.

Compare the two ratios. As you can see, if net profits increase, you get a greater return on your investment.

Take a Moment, page 65

◆ Increased labor costs (hiring contract employees versus hiring employees into the company and providing benefits)

◆ Fluctuating timelines

◆ Need for additional equipment (rented or bought)

◆ Training of new employees versus hiring trained contract employees to do the work

Chapter Review, page 68

1. A liquidity ratio, two of which are the current ratio and the quick ratio. The current ratio looks broadly at the financial performance by comparing current assets and current liabilities, while the quick ratio adds securities that can be quickly turned into cash to the equation. Both help you see how well the business can meet short-term obligations.

2. The ROI increases if net profits increase. It is definitely good.

3. A pro forma financial statement is a projection, or estimate, of what you think future costs and income will be.

4. Choose two of the following:
   a. You can plan ways to collect on accounts receivable.
   b. You can rethink your credit policy.
   c. You can change the price of your product or service so that you are creating more income.
   d. You can plan to get a loan.
   e. You can increase sales.

5. Answers will vary.

Chapter 5

Chapter Review, page 80

1. You will be unable to answer questions effectively, and you are likely to lose your credibility. Employees will take you less seriously. Employees will shut down and quit listening. If it's not important enough for you to understand it, why should they bother?

2. Computer programs, whiteboards or posters in the work area, small groups

3. Look at the employees' developmental level, overall, in regard to financial information. How much do they know about it? Are they likely to ask questions? Do they need training during the information session?

4. Answers will vary.

5. Answers will vary.